HAPPY BENTO!

LUNCHES ON THE GO

ANNA ADDEN

PRAISE FOR HAPPY BENTO

"*Happy Bento* offers 160 pages of lunch box inspiration! In the pages of this book, Anna Adden creates dozens of adorable, creative meals for kids of all ages. Children will love the cute characters and happy scenes, and parents will love the healthful ingredients and entrees that can be quickly thrown together on busy mornings. I can't wait to put some of the ideas in *Happy Bento* to use in my children's lunches!"

— Wendy Thorpe Copley, author of *Everyday Bento: 50 Cute and Yummy Lunches To Go* and publisher of wendolonia.com

"*Happy Bento* offers up delicious inspiration for healthy lunches on the go. Anna's creative approach to packing school lunches, step-by-step instructions, and photo tutorials make packing bento lunches not only fun, but also easy. With this book, you'll discover just how simple it is to create school lunches your kids will look forward to eating every day. A must read for anyone who packs a lunch box!"

– Sherrie Le Masurier, author and founder of schoollunchideas.ca

"As a mother of two, I've learned that kids are more likely to try new foods when they are presented in a fun and engaging way. And if trying new foods is the goal, *Happy Bento* is the answer! In *Happy Bento*, Anna incorporates a variety of nutritious ingredients into all of the lunches, and provides clear instructions for each step. The finished pictures of the bentos, bright and colorful, make me want to reach in and grab a bite! Best of all, *Happy Bento* gives families the perfect opportunity to have a little fun together, both in the kitchen and at the table!"

— Marie H. Saba, mother of two, real-food fanatic, cookbook author, and cooking class instructor

"This bento cookbook, *Happy Bento*, has numerous easy-to-follow recipes which are great for bento beginners. I also loved how the bento recipes are healthy and wholesome with lots of fresh fruits and vegetables. In addition, I would also like to take this opportunity to congratulate Anna on publishing her first book to share her creative ideas on western diet and cute designs for lunch boxes."

— Shirley Wong (Little Miss Bento), bento artist and cookbook author, littlemissbento.com

"*Happy Bento* is full of colorful, creative and healthy kids' lunch ideas. Anna's clear and simple instructions will help you to easily produce an adorable bento lunchbox with a variety of food. Her fun and colorful bento lunches are sure to entice even the pickiest eaters. Your kids will look forward to their lunch box every single day with the wonderful collection of bento recipes in this book."

— Ming, author of *Yummy Kawaii Bento* & bentomonsters.com

ANNA ADDEN

HAPPY BENTO!

LUNCHES ON THE GO

FRONT TABLE BOOKS
AN IMPRINT OF CEDAR FORT, INC. | SPRINGVILLE, UTAH

ISBN 13: 978-1-4621-1664-5

Published by Front Table Books, an imprint of Cedar Fort, Inc.
2373 W. 700 S., Springville, UT 84663
Distributed by Cedar Fort, Inc., www.cedarfort.com

LIBRARY OF CONGRESS CATALOGING-IN-PUBLICATION DATA
    Adden, Anna, 1978-
    Happy bento! / Anna Adden.
        pages cm
    Includes bibliographical references and index.
    ISBN 978-1-4621-1664-5 (acid-free paper)
    1. Lunchbox cooking. 2. Bento cooking. I. Title.
    TX735.A335 2015
    641.5'3--dc23
                        2015009847

Cover design by Rebecca J. Greenwood
Page design by Michelle May and Allison Parrott
Cover design © 2015 by Lyle Mortimer
Edited by Sydnee Hyer

Printed in the United States of America

10   9   8   7   6   5   4   3   2   1

Printed on acid-free paper

CONTENTS

INTRODUCTION

WHAT EXACTLY IS A BENTO? A BENTO is simply a meal packed in a box. It originated in Japan as a means to enjoy a meal on the go. Through the years, bento has evolved into elaborately embellished meals that are pleasing to the eyes as well as the tastebuds. However, a bento can be as simple or complicated as you decide to make it.

I STARTED MAKING BENTO LUNCHES when my daughter began attending preschool. While visiting one of the schools in our area, the topic of lunch came up. How had I not thought about lunch? I started to panic. What in the world will I pack for her? I turned to the Internet and searched preschool lunches. What came up surprised me. Before my eyes were cute, colorful, and fun lunches for kids called bento. I have always been a crafty person, so these lunches appealed to me. I knew it was something that I would have fun making. That is how the bento madness started at my house.

WHY DO I MAKE BENTOS? THE number one reason is because it is fun, both for my kids and for myself. I enjoy making them, and my kids enjoy eating them. Making bentos also encourages healthy eating habits. Arranging food neatly in a bento box or making fun characters out of healthy food entices kids to try new foods. Plus, making bentos at home is cheaper than buying lunch at school or grabbing something from a restaurant on your lunch break. Last but not least, it sends a message that you care. Your loved one knows you spent a little extra time packing lunch. A bento is not just a meal; it is a meal with a side of love.

THIS IS NOT A TRADITIONAL "COOK-book." This is a "how to" book: how to be creative with food and pack it in a box. In this book you will learn the basics of bento making as well as the techniques that I use to make food fun.

BENTO SUPPLIES

MANY DIFFERENT SUPPLIES CAN be used to make a bento. In this section, I will highlight the ones that I use most often. Truth is, you don't really need all of these things. All you really need is a good imagination, a knife, and a box. That's it. However, bento tools can help make the process quicker and easier. The one thing that is a must is a box. This could be a traditional bento box, a lunchbox, or even a simple storage container.

1 JAPANESE BENTO BOXES COME IN A variety of shapes and sizes. The boxes are available in single or multi tiers. These bento boxes vary in cost, anywhere from $1.50 for a plastic bento box all the way up to hundreds of dollars for a wooden, hand-crafted, traditional bento box. Most of the Japanese bento boxes that I own are in the price range of $1.50–$25.

LUNCHBOXES ALL HAVE THEIR OWN unique qualities, so take the time to find the lunchbox that works best for you. They come in an array of sizes and are made from either plastic or stain-

less steel. The price range for these also varies greatly. The most affordable option is EasyLunchboxes, which are $14 for a set of four plastic, divided lunchboxes. The most expensive lunchbox that I own is the PlanetBox Rover, at $60. This lunchbox is a tray-style box made from stainless steel and is built to last. Also significant to note here is that you will need an insulated lunch bag and an ice pack to

keep the food inside these lunchboxes at safe temperatures until lunchtime. Thermoses are also a great option for kids that don't like to eat certain foods cold. Pack the main course in a thermos and pack the sides in a small bento box. There is a new lunchbox coming out called OmieBox, which has a built-in thermos compartment allowing the option to pack warm and cold foods together in one lunchbox.

2 SILICONE CUPS ARE USED FRE-quently in our bento boxes. They can be bent to squeeze into spots in the bento box. Not only do they add a splash of color but they also serve a greater purpose: to keep the wet and dry food items separate. As you will see, the lettuce-shaped silicone cup is my absolute favorite.

3 SAUCE CONTAINERS ARE SMALL containers with lids. These tiny containers are great for packing condiments or dips in. Tiny treats can also be hidden inside these small containers. They add visual interest to the bento box as well.

4 BARAN IS A DIVIDER USUALLY MADE from a plastic sheet or silicone. It helps divide your bento box into sections and keeps food from touching. Baran comes in an array of designs and colors. You are probably most familiar

5

with grass baran, which is used with sushi. Using baran in your bento box is a quick way to add cuteness and color.

5 CUTTERS ARE ESSENTIAL FOR making cute things quickly. Cookie cutters, fondant cutters, vegetable cutters, and sandwich cutters are all readily available. I use them often to make cute sandwiches. Smaller cutters can be used to decorate or add words to sections of the bento.

6&7 PICKS CAN TRANSFORM A lunch from drab to fab in seconds. Japanese bento picks are smaller in size

and are available in countless shapes and themes. Cupcake picks or rings are larger in size and are also available in many themes. Both are great for making your bento cute, and they can double as utensils.

8 EGG MOLDS CAN BE USED TO MOLD a hardboiled egg into a shape. Place the egg in the mold while it is warm. Place the egg mold in ice water or in the refrigerator. Wait a few minutes and presto! A cute, shaped egg that is perfect for your bento.

9 RICE MOLDS ARE TRADITIONALLY used to make onigiri, or rice balls. Add the rice to the mold, press down, and

then pop it out. Decorate the onigiri to look like your favorite character. Traditional onigiri is decorated with nori (dried seaweed).

10 CRAFT PUNCH/NORI punches are great tools to have. It can punch shapes or facial expressions out of nori quickly. A punch can also be used on thinly sliced carrots.

I HAVE ACCUMULATED quite a few bento boxes/lunchboxes since I started making bento. I have used a variety of different ones throughout the book. However, all recipes in this book can be adapted to whichever bento box you have on hand. More information on where to buy bento supplies and bento boxes is in the shopping section located in the back of the book.

CHAPTER 1
BASIC BENTOS

In this chapter I have included many different types of lunches to give you ideas of what can be packed inside your bento box. I try to include vegetables, protein, grains, and fruits in my bentos. Please substitute food items as you see fit for taste preferences. Try to use seasonal fruits and vegetables to keep food costs low.

SANDWICH SUSHI

Give that boring everyday sandwich a new spin. Roll it up to create sandwich sushi.

SUPPLIES

PlanetBox Shuttle, one piece of silicone baran, and knife

INGREDIENTS

Bread, peanut butter, marshmallow fluff, pita crackers, Rainier cherries, mini sweet peppers, and kiwi

DIRECTIONS

TO MAKE THE SANDWICH SUSHI, ROLL the slice of bread flat with a rolling pin. Spread on the peanut butter and marshmallow fluff. Roll the bread up and cut it into three pieces.

PLACE THE PIECES INTO LEFT COMpartment of the bento box. Place the baran separator and then add a handful of pita crackers. Slice and pit the cherries. In the other compartment, add your fruits and veggies. I did them in rows to add visual appeal.

Fully cooked frozen shrimp is another great option for bento boxes. In the morning I rinse off the shrimp and add them to the bento box while they are still frozen. This method helps keep the food cool inside the box, and the shrimp will be thawed before lunchtime.

SUPPLIES
Two-tier, round, stacking bento box (CuteZcute bento box pictured), two pieces of grass silicone baran, and small, lidded dip container

INGREDIENTS
Cooked rice, fully cooked frozen jumbo shrimp, steamed broccoli, strawberries, and cheese sauce

DIRECTIONS
SPOON THE RICE INTO HALF OF ONE OF THE ROUND tiers. Add two pieces of grass baran somewhat over-lapped to stretch the width of the bento box. Add the rinsed frozen shrimp to the other half of the box.

IN THE OTHER TIER, ADD THE STEAMED BROCCOLI and a couple of strawberries. Spoon a little cheese sauce into the small lidded sauce container and add the container between the broccoli and the straw-berries.

SHRIMP & RICE

DIY BENTO LUNCHES

My daughter is particularly fond of this type of bento. She loves being able to have some control and build the items as she wishes. There are many different versions. The ones most packed at our house are mini pizzas and tacos. Other examples are crackers and cheese or sandwich ingredients left unassembled for your child to put together at lunchtime.

MINI PIZZAS

Mini pizzas with toasted English muffins as the crust have long been on the menu. My husband had these growing up. So it's no surprise that they started appearing in our bento boxes.

SUPPLIES

LunchBots Cinco, small round leakproof container, three small square containers with lids, crinkle cutter, and small spoon

INGREDIENTS

One English muffin, tomato sauce (pizza sauce or spaghetti sauce works as well), oregano, baby carrots, orange slices, blackberries, cucumber, sliced olives, shredded cheese, and mini pepperoni

DIRECTIONS

PULL APART THE ENGLISH MUFFIN AND toast the two halves. Spoon tomato sauce into round container, sprinkle with oregano, and place in top right section of box. Place baby carrots in top left section of box. Place orange slices and blackberries in middle top section of box. Slice the cucumber with the crinkle cutter (optional) and place the slices in the bottom of the large right section. Stack the halves of the English muffin in the larger right compartment.

FILL THE THREE SMALL SQUARE CONtainers with the pizza toppings (black olives, shredded cheese, pepperoni). Feel free to substitute any of the toppings for your child's favorites. Line these containers up in the top of the right large sections.

ADD A SPOON SO YOUR CHILD CAN spread the sauce on the mini pizzas. Remember to put the lids on all the containers before you send it off to school.

TACOS

SUPPLIES
ECOlunchbox Blue Water Splash Box, printed wax paper, circle cutter, heart-shaped silicone cup with lid, small round lidded container, rectangle lidded container (mini dipper), spoon, and paring knife

INGREDIENTS
Extra large tortilla, leftover chicken taco filling (chicken, rice, and spices), sliced black olives, two sliced grape tomatoes, shredded cheese, and orange slices

DIRECTIONS

CUT FOUR CIRCLES OUT OF THE EXTRA large tortilla. Place them on the piece of wax paper, staggering them. Fold the paper with the mini tortillas in half and place inside the box. Spoon the taco filling into the heart-shaped cup and place inside the box. Place the sliced black olives and tomatoes inside the mini dipper.

ADD SHREDDED CHEESE TO SMALL round container. Place these two containers in the box. Fill the remaining space with orange slices. Don't forget to add the spoon.

PLACE THE LIDS ON ALL OF THE SMALL inner containers. This bento box has a flexible silicone lid and will bend to accommodate any inner boxes.

Breakfast for lunch is always a hit at my house. My kids love it, and the bento box always comes home completely empty.

SUPPLIES
Stainless steel divided bento box (LunchBots Trio pictured), two small round leakproof containers, and knife

INGREDIENTS
Mini blueberry waffles (fresh or frozen, store-bought or homemade), blueberry yogurt, syrup of your choice, nectarine, and sausage patty

DIRECTIONS
PACK FOUR MINI WAFFLES INTO THE long skinny section. Spoon the blueberry yogurt into one of the round leakproof containers. Pour syrup into the other, slightly smaller round container. Place the containers into the bento box, one in each larger section. Fill the remainder of the spaces with nectarine (or any kind of fruit) on one side, and cut up the sausage for the other.

BREAKFAST FOR LUNCH

PITA CRACKERS & HUMMUS

Another great lunch option for kids is a dipping lunch. Kids love to dip, and hummus is a healthy option.

SUPPLIES

Lego lunchboxes, small rectangle box with lid, and deep silicone cup

INGREDIENTS

Pita crackers, black bean hummus, green grapes, and mini sweet peppers

DIRECTIONS

LINE UP THE PITA CRACKERS IN A ROW on the left side of the box. Spoon hummus into rectangle container and place in box beside the row of pita crackers. Add grapes to the deep silicone cup and add to box. Fill the remaining space with the mini sweet peppers.

I MADE THE SAME LUNCH FOR BOTH of my kids, but with one slight variation for specific taste preferences: I substitute kiwi berries for the grapes in my daughter's bento. Feel free to substitute any of the ingredients for your child's favorites.

HAMBURGER PATTY

Leftovers are another great lunch option, and I am a huge fan of using up leftovers in bentos.

SUPPLIES

Bento box with removable sections (Deli Club bento box pictured), lidded sauce container, and flower bento pick

INGREDIENTS

Leftover hamburger patty with cheese, steamed broccoli, cantaloupe chunks, and cheese sauce

DIRECTIONS

CUT THE LEFTOVER HAMBURGER patty into strips and place in a small section of box. Place the steamed broccoli in the other small section. Add the cantaloupe chunks to the large section. Spoon cheese sauce into lidded container and place in large section. Add the flower pick for a little decoration.

KABOBS

Put it on a stick, and kids will love it. There are so many different food combinations. Anything goes!

SUPPLIES
Yubo lunchbox (only the inner containers are pictured), skewers, heart-shaped silicone cups, paring knife, and mini heart cookie cutter

INGREDIENTS
Pineapple, salami, grape tomatoes, red & yellow mini sweet peppers, red grapes, cheese crackers, applesauce, and red sanding sugar

DIRECTIONS
CUT THE PINEAPPLE INTO CHUNKS and cut the salami slices in half. Push the skewer through the pineapple, rolled salami, and tomato. I cut the tomatoes so they look like little hearts on the skewer. **1** Cut the tomato in half diagonally. **2** Flip one of the tomato halves to make a heart **3** Then skewer.

PLACE THE TWO SKEWERS IN THE sandwich compartment. Add two heart–shaped silicone cups to the sides.

FILL ONE WITH PEPPER RINGS AND THE other with the red grapes. Add cheese crackers to one of the round containers and applesauce to the other one.

SINCE THERE WERE ALREADY HEARTS in this lunch, I decided to decorate the applesauce with a heart by sprinkling red sugar inside a heart-shaped cookie cutter.

I KNOW MOST PEOPLE DON'T HAVE fancy skewers like I do. You can use wood skewers just by trimming them to fit inside your bento box.

Pasta salad is quick and easy to make. Since it is usually served chilled, it's a perfect entrée for a bento box.

SUPPLIES
Bentgo Kids lunchbox and a paring knife

INGREDIENTS
Pasta, grape tomatoes, black olives, mini pepperoni, ham deli meat, olive oil, vinegar, oregano, strawberries, strawberry yogurt, yellow mini pepper, and chocolate-covered blueberries

DIRECTIONS
BOIL THE PASTA UNTIL TENDER, DRAIN, AND RINSE with cold water. Add sliced grape tomatoes, sliced black olives, mini pepperoni, and a slice of ham cut into strips. Pour a small amount of olive oil and vinegar on top, sprinkle with oregano, and mix with your hands. Put the pasta salad in the large compartment.

CUT THE TOPS OFF THE STRAWBERRIES, CUT IN HALF, and add to the upper compartment. Spoon the strawberry yogurt into the right compartment. Cut the mini yellow pepper into pepper rings and add those to the bottom compartment. Last, add four chocolate-covered blueberries to the small circular compartment.

PASTA SALAD

MEATBALLS

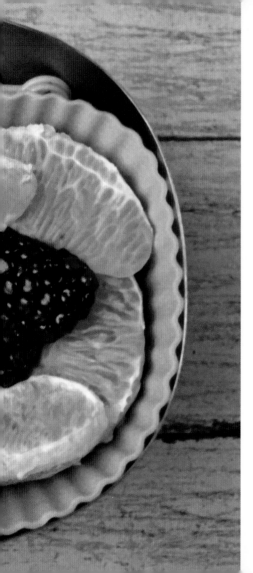

Meatballs from your freezer stash—a great option for those days when the refrigerator is bare.

SUPPLIES
ECOlunchbox Oval, leakproof stainless steel round container, jumbo silicone cup, small fork & spoon, and knife

INGREDIENTS
Meatballs, tomato sauce, oregano, orange slices, blackberries, cheese stick, ginger cookies, and baby carrots

DIRECTIONS
PLACE THE MEATBALLS IN THE ROUND container. Spoon the tomato sauce over the meatballs and sprinkle oregano on top. Stack the orange slices around the side of the silicone cup and add the blackberries in the middle. Place the container and silicone cup into the bento box. Add the cheese stick, utensils, ginger cookies, and baby carrots to the box. I cut the carrots to the same depth of the box.

A Thermos is great for kids who will only eat certain foods warm. Most anything can be packed up in it and kept warm until lunchtime. Pack the sides in a smaller, snack-sized bento box. Our favorites to pack in our Thermos are pasta, soup, and Thai food.

SUPPLIES
Thermos food jar, snack-sized bento box, and ice skate cupcake ring

DIRECTIONS
ADD DESIRED AMOUNT OF LEFTOVER soup to the Thermos jar. To ensure the food is still warm at lunch, follow these steps:

1. Add boiling water to the Thermos and close the lid. Let sit for at least 5 minutes.

2. Heat up the soup (stovetop or microwave) until it is piping hot (hotter than you would serve it).

3. Pour the water out of the Thermos, add your soup, and close the lid tightly.

PLACE SNOWFLAKE CRACKERS AND grapes into snack box. Add the ice skate to the grapes for a little festive fun.

INGREDIENTS
Leftover avgolemono soup (recipe below), snowflake crackers, and green grapes

AVGOLEMONO SOUP (GREEK LEMON, CHICKEN, AND RICE SOUP)
2 cans of cream of chicken soup
1 can of chicken broth
2 baked chicken breasts cut into small pieces
3 cups of cooked white rice
lemon juice to taste (It takes more than you think!)

COMBINE INGREDIENTS IN A POT AND simmer until warm. So yummy!

THERMOS LUNCH

BURRITO

I use burritos frequently in lunches. This has become the sandwich substitute for my daughter. Neat and compact and full of yumminess.

SUPPLIES

ECOlunchbox Blue Water Splash Box, square silicone cup, rectangle silicone cup, lidded sauce container, panda bento picks, and portion cup divider (pictured)

INGREDIENTS

Seasoned cooked beef, rice, beans, shredded cheese, tortilla, broccoli, cherry tomatoes, red grapes, blueberries, and ranch dressing

DIRECTIONS

ASSEMBLE THE BURRITO WITH THE beef, rice, beans, cheese, and tortilla. Slip one end of the rolled-up burrito into the plastic portion cup divider. This will help keep the burrito from coming undone when your child is eating it. Place the burrito in the bento box. Add the broccoli and cherry tomatoes to the rectangle silicone cup. Put the red grapes and blueberries into the square silicone cup and add the panda bento pick. Position them inside the bento box. Add the ranch dressing (or any dip) to the lidded sauce container and set inside the box.

CHAPTER 2

FUN BENTOS

Now that you have mastered
the basics of building
bentos, let's add in some fun.
We are going to amp it up in
this chapter with fun,
kid-friendly, themed bentos.

BLAST OFF

SUPPLIES

Rectangular bento box (book bento box pictured), spaceship cutter, spaceship bento picks, and star-shaped silicone cup

INGREDIENTS

Apple slices, peanut butter, yogurt-covered star cookies, rocket-shaped cheese crackers, blueberries, and blackberries

DIRECTIONS

1 TO MAKE THE APPLE SANDWICHES, slice the apple vertically, as pictured. **2** Use the spaceship cutter to cut out the core. **3** Spread the peanut butter on a smaller apple slice (one that did not contain the core) and top with an apple slice that has the spaceship cutout. Place the apple-wiches in the top section of the bento box. Add a few yogurt-covered star cookies to this section. Put the rocket cheese crackers inside the star-shaped silicone cup. Place this cup in the bottom section. Fill in the empty space around the cup with blueberries and blackberries. For a little more fun, add the spaceship bento picks.

SUPPLIES

Two-tier bento box, hippo cookie cutter, silicone grass baran, knife, chopstick, and hippo bento pick

INGREDIENTS

Soba noodles (recommended, but any noodles will work), butter, salt, candy eye, shelled edamame beans, slice of apple, orange slices, red grapes, and mini red pepper

DIRECTIONS

BOIL WATER AND COOK noodles until tender. I chose the soba noodles for this bento because they had a purple hue and looked like the color of a hippo. Drain the water. Mix a little butter

HIPPOPOTAMUS

and a dash of salt into the noodles. Since noodles will not keep their shape without a mold or cup, I used my hippo cookie cutter as a mold.

PLACE THE COOKIE CUTTER IN THE top tier of the bento box. **1** Put the noodles inside of the cookie cutter. (I curled the noodles around a chopstick to make the nostril.) **2** Add the candy eye and place the shelled edamame beans in the empty space around the cookie cutter. **3** Measure the depth of the box to the top of the cookie cutter with your knife and cut a chunk of apple from your apple slice to that length. Add the piece of apple to the hippo's mouth for his tooth.

ADD THE ORANGE SLICES AND RED grapes to the bottom tier. Place the grass baran beside the grapes. Cut the red mini pepper up into pepper rings then add them to the remaining space in the box. Add the little hippo pick to the grapes.

BUSY BEE

SUPPLIES

ECOlunchbox Oval, round stainless steel container, lettuce-shaped silicone cup, orange scalloped silicone cup, paring knife, bee bento picks, small scissors, nori punches, egg separator, card stock, and pen

DIRECTIONS

START BY SEPARATING THE EGG YOLK from the egg white. Fry the separated egg in a small pan and let cool. **1** While waiting for the egg to cool, draw a bee shape on card stock to use as your template. **2** To do this, draw a circle around the round container onto the card stock to be sure that the bee will be drawn to the correct size. **3** Cut the template into pieces and place the body section on top of the egg yolk and the wings on top of the egg white. Cut around the template with a paring knife.

INGREDIENTS

Egg, bacon, cheddar cheese, English muffin, nori, cream cheese, blueberries, oyster crackers, red pepper, grape tomatoes, and slice of cantaloupe

ASSEMBLE THE BREAKFAST SANDWICH by placing the prepared bacon, remainder of egg, and a slice of cheese inside the English muffin. Put the sandwich inside the round container—if it does not fit in your container, you may need to trim the sandwich some.

4 DECORATE THE BEE WITH NORI strips and punch-outs. I used the bee template again to cut the nori strips to exact size. I also trimmed the smile down with scissors to fit the bee's face. Attach the nori details to the bee with cream cheese. Add the bee to the top of the sandwich using the cream cheese again as the glue. Don't forget to add the antennas above the bee's head. Place round container into the right side of the bento box. Go ahead and put the lettuce silicone cup and orange silicone cup into the box. Add blueberries to the lettuce cup and oyster crackers—"the honeycomb"— to the orange cup. Fill the empty spaces of the box with red peppers and grape tomatoes.

5 NEXT, CUT A SMALL PIECE OF cantaloupe into a beehive shape.

6 ETCH LINES ACROSS THE FRONT with the paring knife. Place on top of blueberries. To complete this bento, add bee picks around the beehive.

DAISY

1

2

3

SUPPLIES

Hello Kitty–shaped bento box, daisy-shaped cookie cutter, small circle cutter, paring knife, lettuce-shaped silicone cup, and ladybug and daisy bento picks

INGREDIENTS

Sandwich bread, deli meat, red and yellow sweet peppers, ginger cookies (I used cat-shaped ones), rocket-shaped cheese crackers, and green grapes

DIRECTIONS

1 CUT TWO SLICES OF BREAD WITH the flower cookie cutter. **2 & 3** Cut a small circle out of the middle of one of the flower slices of bread. Cut the deli meat with the flower cookie cutter, and then assemble sandwich. **4** Cut the bottom off of one of the yellow sweet peppers. **5** Trim the bottom of the pepper with circle cutter. **6** Insert this piece into the hole you cut earlier in the bread. Place sandwich in bento box.

NEXT, SLICE THE YELLOW AND RED peppers into pepper rings. Insert silicone cup into bento box and fill with the pepper rings. Place a small row of ginger cookies above the silicone cup. Next to the cookies, place a small handful of cheese crackers. Now fill the remaining spaces with the green grapes. Lastly, add ladybug and daisy picks for a little extra cuteness.

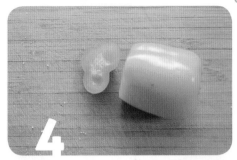

LIONS, TIGERS & BEARS...OH MY!

SUPPLIES
LunchBots Duo, Cuddle Palz cutter set, scalloped vegetable cutter, small circle cutter, food marker, rectangle silicone cup, and bear pick

INGREDIENTS
Seasoned rice, black beans, corn, egg, red pepper, cheese stick, black olives, and green grapes

DIRECTIONS

COMBINE THE SEASONED RICE, BLACK beans, and corn. Spoon mixture into left compartment. Cook the egg in the frying pan. Be sure to break the egg yolk and fry it flat (omelet style). When the egg is done, let cool on cutting board. When cool, cut the egg using the Cuddle Palz tiger plate. Assemble the tiger on top of rice mixture.

1 TO MAKE THE LIONS, CUT THE RED pepper with the scalloped vegetable cutter. **2** Now cut a smaller circle out of the middle. Cut the string cheese into 3 sections. Take one piece and place it into the red pepper. **3** Draw the lion face details on with the food marker.

SLICE THE BLACK OLIVES, PLACE IN rectangle cup, and then add your lions. Fill the remaining space in the bento box with grapes and add a bear pick to complete the theme.

WHAT DOES THE FOX SAY?

A cute little bento based on the viral YouTube video "The Fox" that kids love to sing over and over again!

SUPPLIES

PlanetBox Shuttle, knife, music note picks, and music note cutter

INGREDIENTS

Bagel, cream cheese, strawberry, pineapple, blueberries, strawberry yogurt, and sausage patty

DIRECTIONS

TO START, TOAST HALF OF THE BAGEL. Let cool and then spread the cream cheese on it. **1** Now, dice the strawberry and pineapple into pieces of equal size and width. Next, start arranging the pieces on the bagel into a fox shape. (I used my daughter's perler bead pattern to help with this.) **2** Place blueberries for his eyes, nose, and feet. When completed, place the bagel in the bento box.

FILL THE DIPPING CONTAINER (COMES with the lunchbox) with strawberry yogurt. Use the music note cutter to cut a small strawberry music note and place on top of the yogurt. Cut the sausage into chunks, place in bento box, and decorate with the music note bento picks.

MASHED POTATO PANDAS

Mashed potatoes are easily molded and fun to shape using rice molds or cookie cutters with stamp plates.

SUPPLIES

Single-tier bento box, panda rice mold & panda nori punch (sold as a set on bentousa.com), tweezers, rectangular silicone cup, crinkle cutter knife, and panda bento pick

INGREDIENTS

Mashed potatoes, nori (dried seaweed), strawberries, cucumber, and turkey deli meat

DIRECTIONS

1 SCOOP THE MASHED POTATOES into the rice mold. **2** Press firmly on the back of the mold. **3** Disassemble the mold. Gently ease the mashed potatoes out of the mold (you may need to use a knife). Some of the potato may stick to the mold, but just smooth out those areas of the panda head with your finger.* **4** Place the two panda potato heads in the rectangle silicone cup and then place the cup into your bento box. Use the nori punch to punch the face details out of your nori sheet. **5** Use the tweezers to place the nori details onto the panda's face.

PLACE THE STRAWBERRIES IN A ROW at the back of the box. Cut the cucumber into slices with the crinkle cutter. Place them in a row in front of the strawberries. Cut a slice of turkey deli meat into four even sections and then roll them up. Place the turkey rolls in a row in front of the cucumbers. Add a little panda bento pick to one of the strawberries.

*****ALTERNATIVELY, THE MASHED POTA**toes could be molded in plastic wrap (see method pg. 60) and the nori details cut out of the nori sheet with small scissors.

MICKEY AND MINNIE MOUSE

Sometimes adding a few different decorations can transform the bento from one thing to another. These lunches are an example. It is the same exact lunch done two ways.

SUPPLIES

EasyLunchboxes, Mickey Mouse cookie cutter with stamp plate, Mickey & Minnie Mouse cupcake rings, bow cupcake pick, knife, rolling pin, and melon baller

INGREDIENTS

Sandwich bread, turkey, cheese, condiments (optional), rocket-shaped cheese crackers, red & yellow mini sweet peppers, and honeydew

DIRECTIONS

ROLL THE BREAD SLICES FLAT WITH a rolling pin. Cut out the Mickey Mouse shapes. Press the Mickey Mouse stamp plate into one of the slices. Assemble sandwich with the turkey and cheese. Add condiments if you'd like. Place the sandwich into the box.

ADD THE CHEESE CRACKERS around the sandwich. Core and then cut the sweet peppers into pepper rings, adding to the small compartment. Place Mickey Mouse cupcake ring on top for decorations. Use the melon baller and scoop the honeydew to make the balls then add to last section of the box.

TO TRANSFORM THIS LUNCH INTO A Minnie Mouse lunch, swap out the cupcake ring for the Minnie Mouse one and add a bow cupcake pick to the top of the sandwich.

COOKIE MONSTER

SUPPLIES

Rectangular bento box, Cookie Monster plunger cookie cutter, lettuce-shaped silicone cup, and letter cutters

INGREDIENTS

Sandwich bread, ham, cheddar cheese, condiments (optional), blueberries, mini M&M cookies, grape tomatoes, and slice of cantaloupe

DIRECTIONS

CUT OUT TWO COOKIE MONSTERS from bread with the cookie cutter. **1** Stamp one of the pieces with the plunger. **2** If all the details did not transfer to the bread, put the bread back in the cutter and press with fingers where the details are missing. It's fine if the cutter cuts through some of the bread. Cut the ham and cheese with the cookie cutter. Assemble sandwich. Add condiments if desired.

PLACE THE LETTUCE-SHAPED SILI-cone cup in the box and fill with blueberries. Place three mini M&M cookies on one side of the sandwich and add grape tomatoes in the space on the other side. Use small letter cutters to cut the word "cookie" from the canta-loupe. Spell out "cookie" on top of the blueberries.

HELLO KITTY ONIGIRI

Onigiri, or rice ball, is used in traditional Japanese bento boxes. Rice balls can be shaped and molded into almost anything.

SUPPLIES

Hello Kitty–shaped bento box, lettuce-shaped silicone cup, melon baller, plastic wrap, small scissors, heart-shaped silicone cup, bento picks (Hello Kitty, flower, and bow), and piece of Hello Kitty silicone baran

INGREDIENTS

Sushi rice (any short-grain rice will work), cooked pork, nori, yellow pepper, cantaloupe, grape tomatoes, red pepper, baby carrots, and green grapes

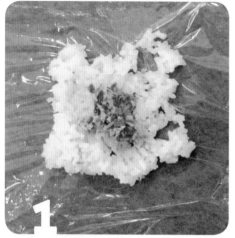

DIRECTIONS

FIRST, MAKE THE PORK-STUFFED Hello Kitty onigiri. Prepare the rice. (I use a rice maker.) **1** Place 2 tablespoons of the cooked rice on top of the plastic wrap. Sprinkle some pork in the middle of the rice.

2 CLOSE THE PLASTIC WRAP AND fold the rice around the pork. **3** Mold the rice into the shape of Hello Kitty™. (I used a Hello Kitty™–shaped cutter to aid in this process.) **4** Place the onigiri into the silicone cup.

CUT 4 SMALL OVALS AND 12 "WHISKers" from the nori shape. Cut two small ovals from the yellow pepper. Decorate the rice balls with the nori and yellow pepper to give the appearance of Hello Kitty™.

PLACE THE BOW PICK IN ONE HELLO Kitty and the flower pick in the other one to complete. Place the silicone cup holding the Hello Kitty onigiri into the bento box.

Next, use the small end of the melon baller and scoop little cantaloupe balls into the heart-shaped silicone cup.

Place that cup into the bento box. Fill in the other spaces with the remaining ingredients (grape tomatoes, red pepper strips, baby carrots, and grapes).

TO FINISH OFF THIS bento, add the Hello Kitty bento pick into the melon balls and a Hello Kitty baran into the grapes.

3

4

ADVENTURES IN WONDERLAND

SUPPLIES

Rectangular bento box with divider, teacup-shaped silicone cup, mini silicone cup, small cat head–shaped cutter, tiny circle cutter, small circle cutter, heart baran, tiny letter stamps, rabbit pick, bottle pick, small diamond-shaped cutter, small heart-shaped cutter, food markers, paring knife, and small scissors

INGREDIENTS

Pineapple, steamed broccoli, chocorooms (mushroom-shaped chocolates), strawberry, tortilla, pepperoni, turkey deli meat, carrots, jack cheese, nori, yellow pepper, red pepper, cheddar cheese, red grapes, and olives

DIRECTIONS

CUT THE PINEAPPLE INTO CHUNKS and put them into the teacup-shaped silicone cup. Add the cup to the bento box. Add the bento box divider next to the silicone cup. Arrange broccoli into a tree shape on the other side of the divider. Put a few chocorooms in the mini silicone cup and place into the bento box in front of the teacup. Cut the strawberry into a heart shape, cut in half, and add to the remaining area in front of the teacup.

NOW, MAKE THE PEPPERONI "ROSE" by cutting a strip from the tortilla.

The width of the tortilla needs to be cut slightly narrower than the slice of pepperoni. **1** Layer the pepperoni on top of the tortilla strip. Let the pepperoni slices hang over one of the edges and then roll it up. Place inside the bento box. Repeat the process, this time using turkey deli meat. Keep the meat flush with the tortilla and secure this roll-up with a rabbit pick.

PLACE THIS ROLL-UP INSIDE THE bento box. Add a stack of black olives in between the two roll-ups. **2** Cut a small piece off of the carrot and stamp

it with the words "eat me." Place the carrot on top of the stack of black olives. Cut the jack cheese with a small circle cutter about the same size as the roll-up. Place the cheese circle on top of the turkey roll-up.

USE THE SMALL SCISSORS TO CUT two small clock hands from the nori sheet. Place the clock hands on top of the cheese circle. **3** Cut a ring from the yellow pepper. Be sure to cut off all the extra bits on the inside to make the pepper ring circular. Place this on top of the cheese clock to complete the clock's face. Add the heart baran behind the roll-ups.

4 PUNCH TINY CIRCLES OUT OF THE red pepper to decorate the broccoli tree with. **5** Add the red pepper "apples" to the broccoli tree, leaving room for the Cheshire Cat's head. **6** Cut the Cheshire Cat from a piece of cheddar cheese and then draw on face details with food markers. Add the Cheshire Cat onto the broccoli tree.

FILL THE EMPTY AREAS OF THE BENTO box with red grapes. Add a bottle pick to the red grapes to represent the "drink me" potion from the story. Cut a diamond and heart out of the red pepper and place each one on a separate chunk of pineapple. **7** Use the same heart cutter to cut a heart shape out of an olive. Place upside down on a pineapple chunk and use a piece of olive scrap as a stem to make a spade.

8 CUT THREE SMALL CIRCLES FROM the olive and add to pineapple to make a club, again using a piece of olive scrap as the stem, and place on top of the last pineapple chunk.

ANGRY BIRDS

SUPPLIES
PlanetBox Shuttle, small square silicone cup, pig plunger cookie cutter, knife, and stem from Angry Birds lip pop

INGREDIENTS
Sandwich bread, turkey, candy eyes, cream cheese, cheese crackers, mini Babybel cheese, carrot, nori, and cucumber

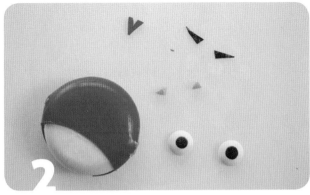

DIRECTIONS

ASSEMBLE SANDWICH AND CUT INTO A triangle shape. Place into large section of box. Use some of the cut-off crust for the eyebrows. Attach eyebrows and candy eyes with cream cheese. Push in the beak (stem of lip pop).* Add cheese crackers to the remainder of the space in that compartment.

1 CUT A SMALL SECTION OF WAX OFF the Babybel cheese. Using the knife, cut a small square from the carrot and then cut it diagonally to make the beak. Cut eyebrows from the nori. **2** Attach eyebrows, candy eyes, and beak with cream cheese. I also used the wax we cut away to make some feathers for the top of the head. Cut a small slit on top of the cheese to insert the wax feathers. Place the finished bird in the square silicone cup and put into bento box.

CUT CARROT AND CUCUMBER STICKS with the knife. Arrange the carrot sticks to form a structure. Take a slice of cucumber and cut and stamp it with the pig plunger cutter. Place into the carrot structure.

***ALTERNATIVELY, CUT A TRIANGLE** from a piece of carrot for the beak and use in place of the lip pop stem.

SUPER MARIO BROS

SUPPLIES

Mushroom-shaped bento box, toothpicks, question mark cutter, knife, stem pick, green silicone cup, lettuce-shaped silicone cup, tiny circle cutter, and small star cutter

INGREDIENTS

Hot dog, cantaloupe, chocolate coin, yellow & red pepper, angel hair pasta, baby carrots, cheese crackers, cream cheese, slice of mozzarella cheese, grape tomatoes, string cheese, and black sesame seeds

DIRECTIONS

CUT A COOKED HOT DOG INTO FOUR pieces. Place them in the green silicone cup. Place the cup in the bottom (larger) tier of the bento box. Cut cantaloupe into squares. Fill the rest of the tier with cantaloupe squares. Slip a chocolate coin beside the green silicone cup.

1 TO MAKE THE PIRANHA PLANT, CUT a section off the red pepper.

2 USE THE TINY CIRCLE CUTTER AND punch holes out of the pepper. **3** Add the teeth by pushing in small pieces of angel hair pasta along the "mouth" of the plant and then add the stem pick. Next, place a couple of carrots in the lettuce silicone cup and place the cup into the upper tier. Add cheese crackers to the empty space. Cut out a question mark from the slice of mozzarella cheese. Place the question mark on top of one of the cheese crackers (you can use cream cheese for the glue).

4 TO MAKE THE MUSHROOMS, SLICE A grape tomato in half and cut two small sections from the string cheese. **5** Assemble these together with a toothpick. **6** Cut tiny circles from the piece of mozzarella cheese and decorate the top of the mushroom. Add black sesame seeds for the eyes. Place the mushrooms into the bento box.

LAST, PUNCH TWO SMALL STARS OUT of the yellow pepper. Place the stars smooth-side down and add black sesame seed eyes.

PAC-MAN

SUPPLIES

PlanetBox Rover, fruit-shaped silicone cups, circle cutters (large and tiny), ghost-shaped cutter (or similar), melon baller, and paring knife

INGREDIENTS

Sandwich bread, slice of cheddar cheese, turkey deli meat, raisins (regular and yogurt-covered), baby carrots, watermelon (or cantaloupe if off-season), grape tomatoes, orange slices, red & yellow sweet peppers, and slice of cucumber

DIRECTIONS

USE THE LARGE CIRCLE CUTTER TO cut two large circles out of the bread and one large circle from the slice of cheese. Assemble the sandwich with the turkey deli meat (add condiments of your choice) but place the cheese on the top of the sandwich. Cut a pie-shaped slice out of the assembled sandwich for Pac-Man's mouth. Add a raisin for his eye. Place sandwich in large compartment.

SPRINKLE RAISINS IN THE TOP COM-partment and then add the yogurt raisins on top to look like the Pac-Man games dots. Cut the baby carrots in half and arrange them in the orange-shaped silicone cup.

POP TWO WATERMELON BALLS IN THE cherry-shaped silicone cups. Place the silicone cups in the lunch box. Fill in the empty areas with grape tomatoes and orange slices.

1 USE THE SMALL GHOST CUTTER AND cut the yellow and red pepper*, can-taloupe, and cucumber with it. **2** If you don't have a ghost cutter, you can improvise by using a small spaceship cutter and cut off the extra bits. Use the tiny circle cutter to cut and/or stamp the ghosts' eyes. Strategically place the ghosts in the lunch box.

*IT IS EASIER TO CUT THROUGH THE pepper if you cut from the flesh side.

SCHOOL BUS SCHOOL BUS SC

CHAPTER 3

SPECIAL DAY BENTOS

FROM BIRTHDAYS TO EARTH
Day, there are plenty of non-
holiday days to celebrate with a
special bento lunch.

BIRTHDAY

SUPPLIES

Monbento original bento box, "Happy Birthday" cupcake pick, balloon cupcake ring, cake sandwich cutter from the Lunch Punch sweets set, small number cutter, and knife

INGREDIENTS

Sandwich bread, American cheese, Monterey Jack cheese, goldfish crackers, carrot, kiwi, and red grapes

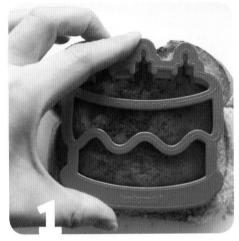

DIRECTIONS

GRILL THE CHEESE SANDWICH AND let cool.* Once cool, use the cake sandwich cutter to cut the sandwich. **1** Gently push down and twist the cutter from side to side until the cutter has completely cut through the sandwich. **2** Use the sandwich cutter to cut the slice of Monterey Jack cheese. (This cutter has staggered plastic edges for cutting and stamping the sandwich.) Be sure to flip the cutter around and press the cheese over all the edges to get all the parts cut out. **3** Cut the candles off the top piece with a knife.

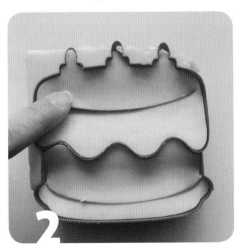

4 USE A NUMBER CUTTER TO CUT OUT the number. Then cut the same number out of a slice of American cheese. Put the yellow cheese number into the blank space in the white cheese. Place the top two sections of cheese on the sandwich to make the frosting. Use the cake cutter to cut out the flames from the American cheese slice and place on top of the candles on the sandwich.

SPRINKLE THE GOLDFISH IN THE bottom of the bento box and place the birthday cake grilled cheese sandwich on top. Then place the bento box divider next to the top of the sandwich. Cut the carrot into sections to fit into the bento box. Cut the kiwi into slices and place into the box. Add red grapes. Slip the balloon cupcake ring over one of the carrots and add the "Happy Birthday" cupcake pick into the grapes.

*TO KEEP THE SANDWICH CRISPY, make the grilled cheese sandwich in the morning. Be sure it is room temperature before adding to the bento box. Pack with other foods that are stable at room temperature. Do not put an ice pack in the lunch bag. Your sandwich will still be crunchy at lunchtime.

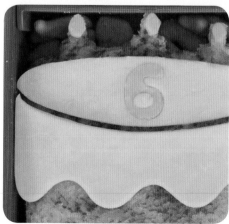

SHARK WEEK

Shark Week is an annual, weeklong event on the Discovery Channel. All week long shark programs are shown on the channel. My son loves sharks, so it's a big deal at our house.

SUPPLIES

Bentgo bento box (I only used the bottom tier), paring knife, small oval cutter, and silicone baran

INGREDIENTS

Wheat bread, ham, mozzarella cheese, blueberries, cream cheese, goldfish crackers, red grapes, and yellow mini pepper

DIRECTIONS

1 TO MAKE THE SANDWICH, FREE HAND cut a rough shape of a shark out of the bread. **2** Then cut an opening for the mouth. Next, cut the fin to be more shark-like. **3** Then take that piece of bread and place on top of the other slice of bread and cut around it (you don't need to cut the mouth out in the bottom piece). Now you have two pieces of bread in the same basic shape.

4 TAKE THE TOP PIECE AND STAMP ON the gills with the small oval cutter. Be sure to only press one side of the cutter into the bread. I made the first two with the long side and then used the narrow end to stamp the last gill. Add the ham and any condiments inside the sandwich. Trim the ham so it is all contained inside the bread.

CUT A STRIP OF CHEESE AWAY AND place the other half inside the sandwich. **5** Cut the teeth out of the cheese by making zigzags with the knife. Be sure to push hard to cut the cheese completely and then pull apart with your fingers. **6** Place this cheese in the mouth of the shark. Add an eye with a blueberry. (I attached it with a dab of cream cheese.)

PLACE YOUR SANDWICH INTO THE bento box. Add goldfish to the space in front of the shark. Place the piece of baran to contain the goldfish. Add a mix of blueberries and red grapes to the rest of the box. Cut the bottom of the mini yellow pepper off and place it in the right upper corner. Then cut four strips from the remaining pepper. Place around the bottom piece to form the sun.

FIRST DAY OF SCHOOL

SUPPLIES

Two-tiered bento box (the one shown has a bus printed on the side), two bus-shaped silicone cups, small scissors, hole puncher, two small rectangle silicone cups, number picks, and mini apple cutter

INGREDIENTS

Macaroni & cheese, nori, regular & alphabet cheese crackers, chicken sausage, yellow tomatoes, and apple

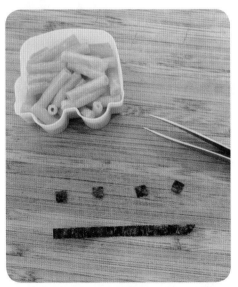

DIRECTIONS

FILL THE BUS SILICONE CUPS WITH THE macaroni & cheese. Cut eight small squares and two lines (the length of the bus) out of the nori paper (pictured left). Punch two holes out of the nori paper with the hole puncher. Place the nori on the mac & cheese with tweezers. Add the buses on both ends of the top tier of the bento box. Fill in the middle area with the regular cheese crackers.

ADD THE ALPHABET CHEESE CRACK-ers (ABC) to the top. Place the two rectangular cups on both end of the bottom tier. Add cut and cooked chicken sausage to the middle. Add yellow tomatoes to one cup and poke the tomatoes with the number picks.

CUT A SLICE OF APPLE AND PUNCH out three small apples with the apple cutter. Place two on the bottom, with the apple flesh showing, and reverse the one on top to show the apple peel.

PICTURE DAY

SUPPLIES
Yubo lunchbox, camera cookie cutter and stamper, knife, happy face cookie cutter, large pink oval silicone cup, and letter cutters

INGREDIENTS
Yellow & red sweet mini peppers, cantaloupe, cucumber slice, orange, turkey deli meat, and tortilla

DIRECTIONS
CORE AND SLICE THREE MINI PEPPERS. Toss into small compartment. Cut a thin slice of cantaloupe from the end of the melon. Cut out and stamp with the camera cookie cutter.

CUT THE SLICE OF CUCUMBER WITH THE happy face cutter. Cut the orange into slices, place into the pink silicon cup, and add the cucumber happy face on top. Place into the large compartment.

LAYER THE TURKEY DELI MEAT ONTO the tortilla and add condiments if desired. Roll up the tortilla and cut into evenly sized pieces. Place into the compartment. Use the letter cutters to punch the word "smile" out of another mini pepper. Place the word on top of the tortilla roll-ups.

TALK LIKE A PIRATE DAY

September 19th is International Talk Like a Pirate Day. This day is increasingly popular to celebrate at school by dressing up as a pirate and talking in pirate lingo.

SUPPLIES
Yumbox Panino, boy sandwich cutter, scissors, tweezers, and ship cupcake pick

INGREDIENTS
Leaf of lettuce, bread, ham, cream cheese, chocolate coins, vanilla yogurt, shark sprinkles, sugar snap peas, baby carrots, red grapes, blueberries, and nori

DIRECTIONS
PLACE THE LETTUCE LEAF INTO THE large compartment. Assemble the sandwich with the ham and cream cheese. Cut, stamp, and seal sandwich with the boy sandwich cutter. Place sandwich on top of lettuce. Place two gold coins by the sandwich.

SPOON THE YOGURT INTO THE CIRCLE compartment. Then place the shark sprinkles in a circle pattern with tweezers. Add sugar snap peas and baby carrots to one of the small compartments and add red grapes and blueberries to the other one.

ADD THE SHIP CUPCAKE PICK TO THE grapes and blueberries. Use the scissors to cut the eye patch and string out of the nori (see picture). Add the nori eye patch to the boy sandwich.

100TH DAY OF SCHOOL

SUPPLIES

Lock & Lock two-tier bento box, number 1 & 0 cookie cutters, apple-shaped silicone cup, crinkle circle cutters, sausage cutters, and hands & heart bento picks (the picks and sausage cutter came together in a set that is sold on bentousa.com)

DIRECTIONS

FILL THE SMALLER COMPARTMENTS OF the box with red grapes, sliced carrot, and blueberries. Cut "100" from your pineapple slices. Place one number in each of the compartments. Next, fill the apple cup with the rice and place into the bento box.

CUT TWO SMALL CIRCLES OUT OF THE corn tortilla (see method pg. 19). Add the seasoned chicken, shredded cheese, and lettuce inside the tortillas and place them inside the bento box. **1** Cut the lil' smokies with the sausage cutter. **2** Add the pick details. Place them on top of the rice. The sausage kids are so happy to be 100 days smarter!

INGREDIENTS

Red grapes, sliced carrot, blueberries, pineapple, seasoned rice, corn tortilla, seasoned chicken, shredded cheese, lettuce, and lil' smokies

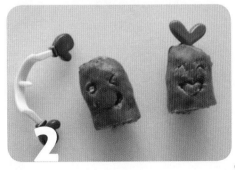

READ ACROSS AMERICA DAY

Read Across America is on March 2nd. This day is widely celebrated in schools across the country. The focus of Read Across America Day is getting kids excited about reading. The day coincides with Dr. Seuss's birthday. This lunch was inspired by the National Education Association's Read Across America Day logo.

SUPPLIES

Laptop Lunches lunchbox, USA-shaped hamburger mold, paring knife, letter cutters, and rectangle silicone cup

INGREDIENTS

Sushi rice, refried beans, lettuce leaf, letter cheese crackers, red bell pepper, red & green grapes, grape tomatoes, and cheese stick

DIRECTIONS

1 SPREAD A THIN LAYER of rice onto the bottom of the USA-shaped hamburger mold* and then spread refried beans in the middle. Now, add some more rice on top. **2** Use the handle plunger and press down. Place the lettuce leaf into the large compartment. **3** Pop the rice out of the mold and place onto the lettuce.

PLACE THE RECTANGLE silicone cup in the bottom of the large compartment. Add the letter cheese crackers to it. Next use the letter cutters to cut the word "read" out of the red bell pepper. Place the word diagonally across the USA-shaped rice. Add green and red grapes to the upper right compartment.

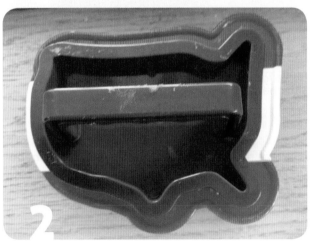

4 COVER THE BOTTOM OF THE LAST container with a single layer of grape tomatoes. Cut the cheese stick to the width of the container. **5** Make stripes starting with a row of grape tomatoes then the cut segment of cheese stick. Repeat till the compartment is filled.

*****USE A USA COOKIE CUTTER IF YOU** don't have a hamburger mold. Alternatively, substitute the rice with a USA-shaped sandwich.

PI DAY

Pi Day is a geeky mathematical day to celebrate the mathematical constant (π). It's celebrated on March 14th, since the date coincides with the pi number. Pie is commonly served this day since it is circular and the mathematical pi is the ratio of the circumference to the diameter of a circle. Confused yet?

SUPPLIES

Large bento box (I used the Smaska lunch box from IKEA), pie-shaped silicone cups, jumbo silicone cup, muffin tin, number picks, dot pick, and paring knife

INGREDIENTS

Refrigerated biscuit dough, frozen mixed vegetables, baked chicken, cream of chicken soup, shredded cheese, slice of jack cheese, blackberries, pineapple, strawberries, grape tomatoes, and red grapes

MINI CHICKEN POTPIES

1 can of refrigerated biscuit dough
2 cups mixed frozen vegetables, thawed
2 cups cubed baked chicken
1 can cream of chicken
shredded cheese to sprinkle on top (optional)

DIRECTIONS

IN A BOWL MIX TOGETHER VEGETAbles, chicken, and soup. Spray the muffin tin with a nonstick baking spray. Press each biscuit into individual cups of the muffin tin. Spoon the mixtures inside and then sprinkle with the shredded cheese. Pinch the tops closed. Bake at 375 degrees for 20 minutes.

PLACE ONE OF THE COOLED MINI chicken potpies into a jumbo silicone cup. Free hand cut a π out of the jack cheese (any white cheese will work). Alternatively, you can make a template first then use that as a guide to cut out the cheese shape (see pg. 41). Insert your potpie into the front of the bento box.

ADD THE BLACKBERRIES, PINEAPPLE chunks, and sliced strawberries into the silicone cups. Place them into the back of the bento box. Fill in the empty areas with grape tomatoes and red grapes. Add the number and dot picks to the grape tomatoes to form 3.14.

EARTH DAY

SUPPLIES

ECOlunchboxes Oval, round lidded leakproof container (comes with the bento box), food coloring, and alphabet picks

INGREDIENTS

Cooked rice, blue food coloring, black beans, shelled edamame, strawberries, broccoli, baby carrots, and yellow sunburst tomatoes

DIRECTIONS

1 COLOR THE RICE BLUE BY USING food coloring. If you are concerned about using food dye, try a natural food colorant or skip this step. **2** Spoon the black beans on the bottom of the round container and **3** then add the blue rice on top. **4** Strategically place the edamame beans to resemble the continents on a globe.*

PLACE THE ROUND CONTAINER INTO the bento box and don't forget to snap on the lid. Fill the remainder of the box with the strawberries, broccoli, baby carrots, and yellow tomatoes. Spell out "earth day" with the alphabet picks.

*ALTERNATIVELY, FOR A WARM MEAL pack the "earth" from the round container into a Thermos and pack a small bento box filled with the other ingredients.

CINCO DE MAYO

SUPPLIES

EasyLunchboxes, Mexican flag pick, sombrero cupcake topper, and mustache pick

INGREDIENTS

Whole-wheat tortilla, refried beans, seasoned rice, shredded cheese, green enchilada sauce, lettuce leaf, candy eyes, green grapes, and mini sweet peppers

DIRECTIONS

ASSEMBLE THE BURRITO WITH BEANS, rice, cheese, and green sauce. Fold up the burrito and cut in half. Place the lettuce leaf in the bottom of the large compartment and place the burrito halves on top. Decorate one half with the sombrero, candy eyes, and mustache pick. (I smeared some refried beans onto the candy eyes to help keep them in place.)

ADD THE GREEN GRAPES AND MINI sweet peppers to the other sections. Poke the Mexican flag into a grape.

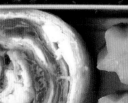

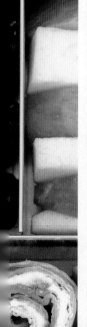

CHAPTER 4
HOLIDAY BENTOS

HOLIDAYS ARE A GREAT TIME TO incorporate bento lunches. If you only want to make an occasional bento, make them around a holiday to make that day so much more special.

NEW YEAR'S DAY

Start off the new year with a fun bento! This bento features "party animal" pizza pockets. I chose the sheep since 2015 is the year of the sheep in the Chinese lunar calendar.

SUPPLIES

Square two-tier bento box (the one pictured looks like a house when stacked), Animal Palz set, top hat pick, letter cutters, alphabet picks, lettuce-shaped silicone cup, and lettuce-shaped silicone baran

INGREDIENTS

Sandwich bread, tomato sauce, oregano, shredded cheese, pepperoni, rocket-shaped cheese crackers, steamed broccoli, cantaloupe, blackberries, and mozzarella cheese

DIRECTIONS

1 TO MAKE THE PIZZA POCKETS, USE the Animal Palz cutter and cut out four pieces of bread. Next, stamp two of the pieces with the sheep plate.* **2** Add the filling (sauce, oregano, shredded cheese, and pepperoni) to the middle

of the bottom slice. **3&4** Press the edges together using the sealer. Then, lightly toast the sandwich to keep the bread from getting soggy.

PLACE THE TOP HAT PICK IN ONE OF THE sheep. Place both pocket sandwiches into the lettuce-shaped silicone cup and place the cup into the top tier. Fill in the remaining space with the rocket cheese crackers. Line the steamed broccoli up in the top part of the bottom tier. Place a piece of lettuce-shaped baran beside the row. Fill in the remaining area with cantaloupe balls and blackberries.

CUT THE WORD "HAPPY" FROM THE mozzarella cheese and place on top of the broccoli. Poke the alphabet picks into the cantaloupe to spell out "New Year."

*TIP - TO MAKE THE BREAD MORE PLI-able, warm it up in the microwave for a few seconds before you stamp it.

GROUNDHOG DAY

INGREDIENTS

Pancake, raw piece of angel hair pasta, raisins, two grains of cooked rice, syrup, bacon, green grapes, and cantaloupe

SUPPLIES

LunchBots Duo, Easylunchboxes mini dipper, Cuddle Palz set, lettuce-shaped silicone cup, silicone flower baran, flower picks, melon baller, silicone grass baran, and snowflake cupcake pick

DIRECTIONS

CUT THE PANCAKE WITH THE CUDDLE Palz cutter. Stamp the cutout with the bear face plate. **1&2** Cut off the ears and then use the inner ear cutter of the hamster plate to cut the ears. Attach

3

the ears with two small pieces of angel hair pasta. **3** Add raisin into the facial cut out areas. Flatten the raisin for the nose and then cut with the nose part of the bear cutter. Add two grains of cooked rice for the teeth. **4** Place the pancake scraps in the bottom of the lettuce silicone cup and place into bento box. The finished groundhog is placed on top of the scraps.

NEXT, PUT THE MINI DIPPER BESIDE the pancakes and add syrup. This is his "shadow." Tear the strip of bacon into

4

two pieces and tuck in above the mini dipper. Place the green grapes on the right bottom and add the grass baran beside them. Scoop out cantaloupe balls and place in the empty area.

NOW ADD THE FLOWER BARAN AND flower picks to the cantaloupe to represent the early spring. Add the snowflake cupcake pick to the grapes to represent six more weeks of winter.

VALENTINE'S DAY

SUPPLIES
Divided lunch box, heart cutters with stamps, small rectangle silicone cups, heart picks, and tiny heart cutter

INGREDIENTS
Red grapes, fresh pineapple, cookie butter, rice cake, shelled edamame, baby carrots, and mini Babybel cheese

DIRECTIONS

PUT THE RED GRAPES INTO THE smaller section. Cut slices from the pineapple. **1** Use the heart cutters to cut the slices into hearts. **2** Then stamp on the words. You'll need to press hard to leave the impression.

ALTERNATIVELY, LEAVE THE HEARTS plain or cut letters from a pepper and add to the hearts. Smear the cookie butter (it's Valentine's day after all!), into a heart shape on the rice cake. (Any spread your child enjoys will work, including peanut butter, Sunbutter, Wowbutter, Nutella, chocolate, and so on.)

PLACE THE RICE CAKE INTO THE BOX. Add the shelled edamame to the rectangle cups. Cut the baby carrots diagonally and then pin them together with the heart picks to form hearts (see method pg. 26). Place them on top of the edamame and then place the cup below the rice cake.

CUT OUT TWO SMALL HEARTS FROM the edge of the Babybel cheese. You may need to use a knife to remove the wax. Place the Babybel cheese inside the lunchbox.

ST. PATRICK'S DAY

SUPPLIES

Lego lunchbox, rectangle inner container, square inner container, lidded sauce container, and pot-of-gold cupcake pick

INGREDIENTS

Sugar snap peas, baby carrots, green grapes, steamed broccoli, jalapeño cilantro hummus, and pita bread

DIRECTIONS

STACK THE SUGAR SNAP PEAS AND baby carrots on the right side of the box. Place green grapes inside the square inner container and place inside the bento box. Add the steamed broccoli. Spread the hummus on the pita bread and roll up. Cut into three pieces, place inside rectangle container, and insert into the box.

ADD HUMMUS TO THE LIDDED CONtainer and place on top of the snap peas to be used as dip for the vegetables. Add the pot-of-gold cupcake pick to the green grapes.

EASTER

SUPPLIES

Rectangular bento box, bunny sauce container, baby chic egg mold, Easter egg cupcake ring, bunny mini cutter, "Happy Easter" cupcake pick, lettuce silicone cup, and silicone eggshell egg poacher

INGREDIENTS

Spring lettuce mix, hard-boiled egg, strawberries, red grapes, pineapple slice, baby carrots, and salt

DIRECTIONS

PLACE THE SILICONE EGGSHELL EGG POACHER INTO the bento box. Add a little spring salad mix to the bottom to the cup. Place molded hardboiled egg inside (see molding hardboiled egg method pg. 123).

SLICE TWO LARGE STRAWBERRIES AND ADD TO THE bento box under the eggshell cup. Add the lettuce cup next to the strawberries. Fill the cup with red grapes. Cut three small bunnies from a pineapple slice and place on top of the grapes. Place the baby carrots in the remaining area.

ADD THE CUPCAKE TOPPERS FOR DECORATION (Easter egg and "Happy Easter"). Add a small pinch of salt to the sauce container.

INDEPENDENCE DAY

SUPPLIES
LunchBots Trio, knife, small star cutter, and star cupcake pick

INGREDIENTS
Blackberries, apple, lemon juice, cream cheese, tortilla, strawberry jam, and yellow carrot

DIRECTIONS

PLACE A HANDFUL OF BLACKBERRIES into the upper left section. Cut the apple into slices. **1** Brush lemon juice on the slice to keep apples from browning. Place the apple slice in the other large section, alternating the skin and flesh showing to create stripes.

SPREAD THE CREAM CHEESE ONTO the tortilla and then spread the jam. Roll the tortilla up. Cut into sections, measuring the depth of the bento box. Add three pieces to the long, skinny section.

CUT PIECES OF CARROT TO THE DEPTH of the bento box. **2** Push the pieces of carrot through the star cutter and then add to the bento box. Add a star cupcake pick to the blackberries.

HALLOWEEN

SUPPLIES
Laptop Lunches lunchbox, bat cutters
(2 sizes), Animal Palz set, coffin cookie
cutter, gravestone cupcake pick, and
red silicone cup

INGREDIENTS
Halloween-shaped tortilla chips
(available at Cost Plus World Market),
carrot, salsa, chocolate chips, raspberries, egg, and cheese stick

DIRECTIONS

ADD A HANDFUL OF HALLOWEEN TOR- tilla chips to one of the large compartments, making sure the bat-shaped ones are on top. Cut two small bats and one larger one from the carrot. Spoon salsa into a smaller compartment and add the carrot bats on top.

PLACE THE COFFIN CUTTER INSIDE THE other large compartment. Stuff the chocolate chips inside the raspberries and place them inside the coffin. Add the gravestone cupcake pick.

BOIL THE EGG FOR 15–20 MINUTES. Take hot egg out of water and peel under cold water. **1** Assemble the Animal Palz mold. **2** Take the egg and place inside the egg mold. **3** This mold slides sideways into the cutter to keep pressure on the egg as it is cooling. Place the mold with the egg inside into the refrigerator for 5 minutes. Take egg out of the mold and place inside red silicone cup and pop into the bento box.

DRAW A WOODEN STAKE ONTO THE cheese stick wrapper and then place into the long skinny section.

THANKSGIVING

SUPPLIES
Yubo lunchbox, dumpling press, rolling pin, kitchen scissors, food markers, and alphabet cutters

INGREDIENTS
Sandwich bread, tomato sauce, oregano, cheese, uncooked angel hair pasta, apple chunks, red grapes, and raspberries

DIRECTIONS
1 PLACE YOUR PIECE OF BREAD ONTO THE DUMPLING PRESS. FLATTEN OUT THE middle area (where the toppings will go) with your fingers. **2** Add the pizza filling

(tomato sauce, oregano, and cheese) to the middle.* **3-5** Pinch closed with the dumpling press. Toast the bread to avoid it getting soggy.

6 WITH THE SCISSORS, CUT OUT three turkey head shapes from the remaining bread. **7** Draw on turkey features with the food markers. Attach the heads to the bodies with a small piece of angel hair pasta.

ADD THE TURKEY PIZZA POCKETS TO the large container. Make a small fruit salad by mixing the apple chunks, red grapes, and raspberries together. Pour into the small container and add the alphabet picks to spell out "gobble."

*DO NOT OVERFILL. THIS WILL CAUSE the bread to break.

CHRISTMAS

SUPPLIES
Monbento square bento box, small tree cutter, candy cane cupcake pick, Christmas bulb ornament cupcake pick, jumbo red silicone cup, and regular-sized green silicone cup

INGREDIENTS
Cheese tortellini (Christmas colors), mozzarella cheese, green grapes, and grape tomatoes

DIRECTIONS
ADD THE COOKED TORTELLINI TO THE inner container of the bento box. Cut out three small trees from the mozzarella cheese and add them on top of the tortellini. Add a handful of grapes to the jumbo silicone cup and place in bento box. Add grape tomatoes to the green silicone cup and place in remaining area. Add the candy cane and Christmas bulb cupcake picks for decoration.

CHAPTER 5

SEASON BENTOS

WE ALWAYS WELCOME THE FIRST DAY
of a new season with a bento lunch
inspired by that season.

SPRING

SUPPLIES

Bento box with removable compartments, flower-shaped silicone cup, stem bento pick, ladybug pick, butterfly pick, melon baller, flower-shaped vegetable cutter, rectangular silicone cup, flower-shaped egg molds (daisy & tulip), peeler, and natural food coloring

INGREDIENTS

Carrot, eggs, green beans, blueberries, and cantaloupe

DIRECTIONS

1 PEEL STRIPS FROM THE CARROT. Boil water and add eggs, green beans, and carrot strips. Only cook the carrot strips for a couple of minutes.
2 Remove the carrot strips from the water, let cool, and roll up. Add the stem pick to one of the roll ups.

REMOVE THE GREEN BEANS WHEN they are cooked to your liking. **3** Bend to fit in the bottom of the flower cup. Add the carrot roses on top and place into the white compartment. Fill the rest of the space with the blueberries. Add the ladybug and butterfly pick for cuteness. **4** Take the hardboiled

eggs out of the mold. (See pg. 123 for how to mold hardboiled eggs.) **5** Place the tulip egg in the natural food coloring and let sit until desired color is achieved. **6** Cut the center of the daisy-shaped egg out to let the egg yolk show. Place the eggs in the green rectangle silicone cup.

USING THE SMALL END of the melon baller, scoop the cantaloupe to fill the remaining space. I also added a couple of flower-shaped melon pieces.

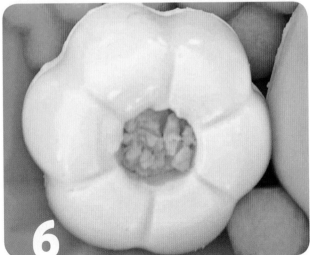

SUMMER

SUPPLIES

Monbento tresor box, sunglasses cupcake pick, toothpicks, peeler, small scissors, knife, letter cookie stamps, and palm tree picks

INGREDIENTS

Carrot, breaded baked chicken strips, cantaloupe, blueberries, and red bell pepper

DIRECTIONS

USE THE PEELER TO PEEL A SMALL piece from the carrot. Cut with scissors to resemble a surfboard shape. Stamp "summer" onto the surfboard with the letter stamps.

ARRANGE CHICKEN STRIPS ON THE bottom tier. Add palm tree pick. Add melon balls and blueberries to one of the side dish containers.

CUT FIVE SMALL TRIANGLES FROM THE remaining cantaloupe. Attach the triangle to one of the cantaloupe balls with pieces of toothpick to form the sun.

SLICE THE BELL PEPPER AND ADD TO other side-dish container. Top off with the sunglasses pick.

FALL

SUPPLIES
PlanetBox Rover, leaf-shaped pastry cutters, leaf-shaped mini cookie cutters, peeler, leaf craft punch, and small square silicone cup

INGREDIENTS
Sandwich bread, turkey, sweet mini peppers, soft chocolate, fig cookies, edamame, green grapes, oranges, strawberries, and carrot

DIRECTIONS

PUNCH THE LEAF SHAPES OUT OF bread with the leaf cutters. Add turkey, assemble sandwiches, and place into box. Cut the mini peppers with the different mini cookie cuter leaf shapes. Add to box.

CUT THE SOFT CHOCOLATE WITH THE mini maple leaf cutter. Add two fig cookies to the square silicone cup and place into the lunchbox. Fill the remainder of that compartment with edamame. Next make the fruit salad with the grapes, oranges, and strawberries.

1&2 PEEL THIN SLICES FROM THE carrot and place them in the craft punch. **3&4** Punch out leaf shapes. Sprinkle on top of the fruit salad.

WINTER

SUPPLIES
Yumbox Panino and snow globe cookie cutter

INGREDIENTS
sandwich bread, ham, cheddar cheese, holiday pretzels, yogurt-covered raisins, peach yogurt, sugar snowflakes, and orange slices

DIRECTIONS
CUT AND STAMP THE BREAD. ASSEMble sandwich and place inside the large compartment. Add pretzels around the sandwich. Put the yogurt raisins in the small compartment. Add the yogurt to the top right comparment and decorate with blue sugar snowflakes. Place orange wedges in the remaining compartment and decorate with the white sugar snowflakes.

SHOPPING

By now you are probably wondering where to find all of these fun little bento supplies. I have been making bentos for over three years now and have accumulated quite the bento stash. Shopping for bento supplies is just as fun as making a bento. My number one go to place is BentoUSA (www.bentousa.com). Everything bento related can be found there: bento boxes, bento picks, cups, baran, cutters, egg molds, etc. Other online resources are listed on pg. 147.

KITCHEN STORES (Williams-Sonoma, Sur La Table, Kitchen Collection) are great to scour, especially when they have a sale. Some things you can find at a kitchen store that can be repurposed for bento are cookie cutters, fondant cutters, food markers, cupcake sets, Zoku cutter sets, and cake pop molds.

CRAFT STORES (Michaels, JoAnn Fabric, Hobby Lobby) carry cookie cutters, fondant cutters, silicone cups, silicone molds, and cupcake toppers. Don't forget that coupons are available to use at these craft stores!

DISCOUNT STORES (Home Goods, TJ Maxx, Ross, Marshalls, Christmas Tree Shops, Tuesday Mornings) have a kitchen and baking aisle. I have found fun seasonal silicone cups in cupcake sets here before. I have even found bento boxes at these stores! Also, they usually carry colorful, fun-shaped pasta, which is great for bentos.

COST PLUS WORLD MARKET is another great store to find tools to use for making bento. I have found tiffin boxes (metal boxes with latches similar to bento boxes), silicone cups, and great seasonal picks and molds there. They also carry imported food that is fun to include in bentos from time to time.

TARGET and WALMART carry cookie cutters, sandwich cutters, silicone cups, and even an occasional bento box. Always check the dollar section, and be sure to stop by around a holiday and check the seasonal aisle for fun new things.

If you live in a larger city, check to see if there is a CAKE BAKING AND DECORATING SUPPLY STORE in your area. These stores carry cupcake picks and rings that are great for decorating a bento.

I have been seeing more things pop up at the GROCERY STORE—cute snack cups, sandwich cutters, and cupcake kits. Check with the baking department, as some grocery stores will allow you to purchase just the cupcake toppers.

A DOLLAR STORE (Dollar Tree, 99 Cents Only Store) is another great place to find things. Holiday cupcake sets with plastic cupcake picks, snack cups, and lip pops (use the plastic stem for bento decorations) can be found there.

PARTY SUPPLY STORES (Party City, Party Depot, Oriental Trading Co.) are great places to find themed cupcake picks. With a little ingenuity, bento supplies can be found almost anywhere.

ONLINE SHOPPING

www.bentousa.com

www.bentoandco.com

www.jbox.com

www.akazuki.com

www.amazon.com

www.ebay.com

www.orientaltrading.com

BRICK AND MORTAR SHOPS

DAISO JAPAN - Los Angeles, San Diego, San Francisco, and Seattle

ICHIBAN KAN - San Francisco

JAPANESE MARKETS - Marukai Market, Mitsuwa Marketplace, Nijiya Market.

LUNCH BOXES

LUNCHBOTS

www.lunchbots.com *

EASYLUNCHBOXES

www.easylunchboxes.com *

PLANETBOX

www.planetbox.com *

ECOLUNCHBOXES

www.ecolunchboxes.com *

MONBENTO

www.monbento.com *

YUBO

www.getyubo.com *

LAPTOP LUNCHES

www.laptoplunches.com *

MARIUS LUNCH BOX

www.uglycc.com

BENTGO

www.bentgo.com *

YUMBOX

www.yumboxlunch.com *

OMIEBOX

www.omielife.com

* also available for purchase on Amazon

BE CREATIVE & HAVE FUN!